Cyber crime

Face the Facts
# Cyber Crime
Neil McIntosh

For information, address the publisher:
Raintree, 100 N. LaSalle, Suite 1200 Chicago, IL 60602

Produced by Monkey Puzzle Media
Design by Mayer Media/Jane Hawkins
Originated by Dot Gradations Ltd
Printed and bound in China.

07 06 05 04
10 9 8 7 6 5 4 3 2

**Library of Congress Cataloging-in Publication Data**
McIntosh, Neil, 1974-
    Cyber crime / Neil McIntosh.
        v. cm. -- (Face the facts)
    Includes bibliographical references and index.
    Contents: What is cyber crime? -- The growth of cyber crime -- Cyber crime in society -- The debate about cyber crime -- What is being done? -- Cyber crime and you -- Facts and figures.
    ISBN 0-7398-6432-7 (Library Binding-Hardcover)
    1. Computer crimes--Juvenile literature. [1. Computer crimes.] I. Title. II. Series.
    HV6773 .M39 2003
    364.16'8--dc21

                            200201285

**Acknowledgments**
The publishers would like to thank the following for permission to reproduce photographs:
p. 5 Mark Edwards/Still Pictures; p. 6 Rex Features; p. 7 Sam Ogden/Science Photo Library; pp. 8, 10, 13, 16, 21, 32; Reuters/Popperfoto; p. 9 Henry Diltz/Corbis; p. 12 Gene J. Puskar/Associated Press; pp. 14, 15 ABC News/Associated Press; p. 17 Ed Wray/Associated Press; p. 18 Jim Cole/Associated Press; p. 19 Damien Dovarganes/Associated Press; pp. 20, 29 Koji Sasahara/Associated Press; p. 22 Ariel Skelley/Corbis StockMarket; pp. 24, 26, 28, 46, 50 Corbis; p. 31 Ron Edmonds/Associated Press; pp. 32, 34, 36 Toby Talbot/Associated Press; pp. 34–35 Digital Vision; p. 37 Daymon J. Hartley/Associated Press; p. 38, 39 Ted S. Warren/Associated Press; p. 40 Shizio Kambayashi/Associated Press; p. 43 William Philpott/Associated Press; p. 45 MGM/UA/Kobal Collection; p. 49 Tim Mayer.

Cover photograph reproduced with permission of Photodisk.

Every effort has been made to contact copyright holders of any material reproduced in this book. Any omissions will be rectified in subsequent printings if notice is given to the publishers.

Some words are shown in bold, **like this.** You can find out what they mean by looking in the Glossary.

# Contents

# A New Kind of Crime

It is easy to imagine crime as we see it in movies: masked gunmen breaking into a building at night, stealing money from under the noses of sleeping security guards, and ending up in a big car chase with the police. Of course, in the movies the police almost always catch up with the bad guys and make an arrest, and the crooks are sent to jail.

However, there is a new kind of crime that is not so easy to see. There are no dramatic raids, no shoot-outs, and no rubber masks. This is a world where the "bad guy" can be thousands of miles away from his victim. This is cyber crime, a crime carried out using computers.

Using computers to commit a crime doesn't make it any less serious than "real world" crime. Huge amounts of money can be stolen, big businesses can be brought to a halt, and illegal information can be swapped. It does mean, however, that criminals can live far away from their targets, and never need to leave their homes to commit their crimes.

## How does cyber crime happen?

Everyone knows that computers are very important to people and their businesses. That is why buildings that house banking computer systems are usually very secure, with high fences outside, no windows, guards on the premises, and complicated entry systems to let workers in and out.

The problem is that in order to work properly, many of these computer systems must be allowed to talk to other computer systems. For example, if someone buys a book over the Internet, their computer is talking to another computer that might be sitting in a secure, carefully guarded building. The weakness is not in the real world, where you would not be allowed into the building even if you were buying a book from one of the computers inside. The weakness lies in the "virtual," or "cyber" world, a world made up of phone lines and computer connections.

Cyber criminals do not attack buildings, they attack computers, and they get at the computers over the same links we use every day when we make telephone calls, send e-mail, or surf the **World Wide Web.**

5

# What Do Cyber Criminals Do?

## Theft and fraud

What are cyber criminals doing when they break into computer systems? The most obvious crime is stealing money. Cyber criminals have found ways to use other people's **credit cards** without their knowing about it and without ever having seen the card itself. They have also managed to persuade banks' computers to transfer money to them, and have ordered goods and services without paying for them.

Other cyber criminals try to steal commercial secrets. These secrets might be taken for the thief's own use, or perhaps for someone else who is paying them. A big problem is when employees themselves turn into cyber criminals, and break into their own company's computer systems to damage important files or steal secrets. They might do this because of a grudge against a co-worker or boss.

There are also people who, rather than break into computers themselves, design computer **viruses** that cause damage automatically. Virus creators are usually computer programmers who want to show off their skills. They get satisfaction by outwitting the makers of antivirus software, which is designed to keep crimes such as this from happening.

## Illegal communication

Another group of cyber criminals tries to distribute illegal information. This may include racist material. For example, there are websites that encourage people to attack or take other illegal actions against particular groups in society. Other sites might sell or pass on certain types of illegal **pornography.** Police and child protection groups are particularly worried about sites featuring indecent pictures of children, and about other sites that allow children access to adult material.

There is also deep concern about information exchanged between terrorists over the Internet, such as detailed "recipes" for making bombs. The problem for police forces around the world is that much of this material—from racist literature to bomb recipes—is not illegal everywhere: countries around the world have different laws.

## Sharing music

Perhaps the most widespread kind of cyber criminal is the ordinary computer user. Trading commercial music files (known as **MP3s**) is very popular among some music fans, but it is also a kind of theft, and is illegal in nearly every country in the world.

The spread of music-swapping services has been a big problem for the music industry, because many Internet users are listening to music that they have not paid for. This means that music companies, and the recording artists themselves, are having their work stolen. There have been court cases, mostly in the United States, aimed at closing down music-sharing services.

If you include all those who download illegally copied MP3s, there are millions of cyber criminals around the world. It is just the seriousness of the crime that varies.

# The First Cyber Criminals

Cyber crime might sound like a very new type of crime, but it has been around since the early 1970s, before the **personal computer** was invented. Then, computers that were far less powerful than today's game consoles filled entire rooms and were looked after by technicians who wore white coats.

## Phone "phreaking"

The first cyber crimes were carried out across telephone lines by a group of electronics enthusiasts known as "phone phreakers." They had studied the U.S. telephone system and realized it used a series of musical tones to connect calls. They found they could imitate those tones and steal free phone calls by creating small musical devices called "blue boxes." One famous phreaker, John Draper, even discovered that using a whistle given away inside a cereal box could do the same job as a blue box. He was nicknamed "Captain Crunch," after the cereal.

Draper became very serious about taking advantage of the weaknesses in the U.S. telephone system. He drove around the country in a large van packed with equipment, taking it to remote spots where he could plug into the telephone network and make illegal, free calls around the world.

Draper became an important influence to two young men, Steve Jobs and Steve Wozniak. They would later go on to found Apple Computer, one of the first personal computer companies. However, in the early 1970s, they were fascinated by phreaking after reading a magazine article about Draper and his activities.

Jobs and Wozniak built a blue box to let them make free long-distance calls, just like Draper. When they tried it out at a phone booth they were caught by passing police officers, and only escaped by telling them that the device was a musical instrument. Despite this close call, they met up with Draper and the three continued to experiment. One time they even made an illegal call from California to the Vatican City in Rome.

## Going straight

After a while Jobs and Wozniak became worried that they would eventually be caught. The two moved out of phreaking and into computing, where they turned the technical skills they had developed building the blue boxes to building computers. They both became millionaires. Draper, on the other hand, was not so sensible. He was caught phreaking, found guilty of **defrauding** the telephone company, and thrown in jail. He has since reformed. Draper now runs a computer security company that protects businesses from **hackers,** who try to break into computers.

# The Growth of Cyber Crime

For many years after Draper and Wozniak started making their blue boxes, cyber crime stayed centered on the telephone. The goal was to get free or cheap telephone calls. The first known computer-to-computer cyber crime did not happen until the 1980s.

## The role of the Internet

It was the arrival of the Internet that eventually made cyber crime a big issue. The Internet linked together lots of small computer **networks** into what is known as the **World Wide Web.** For the first time, computer users could "talk" to each other directly.

The early cyber criminals were helped by ordinary computer users' lack of understanding of the power of the Internet. For most people cyber crime was not a concern. **Hackers** were thought to be relatively harmless kids and were even glamorized in the 1984 film *Wargames*, where a hacker (played by Matthew Broderick) saves the world.

The Internet was originally created and used by the Department of Defense during the 1960s. It was then primarily used by university and government research organizations. It seemed unlikely that people at these institutions would want to damage the network. Because access was more or less limited to the people who developed the Internet, there seemed to be no need to take precautions against cyber crime.

When Internet access extended to millions of homes and businesses in the early to mid-1990s, there were still very few people who were thinking about the dangers of cyber crime and ways of preventing it. Banks and other big businesses were much more interested in the benefits that computer networks could bring them than in any possible dangers.

## Security flaws

For these reasons security was sometimes very basic. People who were experts on how the Internet worked were often able to find a way around these simple protective measures, even on the most important computer networks.

Besides the risk from hackers, very few of the new Internet users were thinking about the threat of **viruses.** Today viruses have become a concern for almost all computer users.

The Internet has made it possible for people to communicate over great distances quickly and inexpensively. Laws have had to change, or be specially created, to protect people from criminals while also protecting free speech.

# The Rise of the Virus

These are members of the computer Emergency Response Team that fought the Melissa virus outbreak in Pittsburgh in 1999.

When we get sick, it can be because we have caught a bug, or **virus,** from someone else—perhaps a friend or member of our family. Computers can get viruses too, and they spread from computer to computer, much like a human illness. Through the Internet, one infected computer can spread the virus to many thousands of other computers.

## What is a computer virus?

Computer viruses are small computer programs that can spread to other computers through an infected disk or attached to an e-mail. Some viruses are harmless, and are not designed to do anything other than copy itself onto other users. Other viruses are designed to pop a message on the screen on a particular date, although these viruses can accidentally cause other problems if they are not well programmed.

Increasingly, though, viruses are being created that are deliberately more damaging, destroying files and even entire disks, and carrying out **Denial of service (DOS)** attacks on other machines on the Internet. DOS attacks are when computers around the Internet send lots of messages to a single target computer. The target cannot cope with all the messages, and stops working. The most successful DOS attacks have caused some parts of the Internet to temporarily stop working.

# The Melissa virus

One of the earliest serious computer viruses was named "Melissa" by its creators. It struck in March 1999, and targeted users of **software** made by Microsoft. The vast majority of computers use at least some Microsoft software. When a user "caught" the virus, an infected e-mail would be sent to the first 50 people on the user's e-mail address book without the user knowing about it. It was not designed to cause problems, but the huge rise in the number of e-mails being sent (50 from every infected user) meant that parts of the Internet quickly became jammed.

David Smith, a 30-year-old programmer from New Jersey, was eventually arrested. He pleaded guilty to causing over $80 million in damage.

Since Melissa, many more viruses have been let loose. All of them have been dealt with, but the costs have been high. Some people worry that one day a cyber criminal will create a virus that could halt the entire Internet. This could cause companies to lose huge amounts of money, and in turn, cause people around the world to lose their jobs.

David Smith stands trial in a New Jersey courtroom.

# Cyber Crime Overview

## Fraud

Cyber crime started with **fraud.** The first person to be found guilty of cyber crime on a computer was Ian Murphy (known as "Captain Zap"). In 1981 he broke into a U.S. telephone company's computer and changed the internal clock so that customers were given cheap phone calls at peak times.

Hacking gained public awareness during the mid-1980s due, in part, to the movie *Wargames.* Many hackers later said that the hit movie was their inspiration.

As hacking grew in popularity, phone companies were, typically, still the victims. Kevin Mitnick was jailed in 1989 for breaking into a phone company computer system. In 1993 three hackers were found guilty of hacking into a telephone company so they could win a radio station phone-in competition. They "won" $20,000 in cash, two sports cars, and vacations in Hawaii before police caught up with them.

It was only a matter of time before banks became the new target; and in 1994 it happened. A group of Russian hackers broke into Citibank's computers and stole $10 million. That said, the gang's ringleader was quickly caught, and all but $400,000 of their haul was recovered.

With the rise of the Internet, **credit cards** became tools of cyber criminals. Kevin Mitnick was arrested (again) for stealing 20,000 credit card numbers over the Internet in 1995. Crimes such as this have prompted credit card companies to consider ways they can make cards more secure for their customers.

## Viruses

At first **viruses** were spread by disks being passed between computers. The Michelangelo virus of 1991 was this type of virus. It was programmed to wipe out **hard drives** on the birthday of the famous Italian painter it was named after.

Now viruses are usually spread over the Internet. There are many viruses around, but famous ones include the "Melissa" virus in 1999, and the "ILOVEYOU" virus of 2000. In 1995 a British man named Christopher Pile became the first person to be jailed for writing a virus.

## Terrorism

Following the terrorist attacks on New York and Washington in 2001, terrorism over the Internet became a new fear. After those attacks it was discovered that the planners could have been communicating by e-mail. In the United States, new laws were introduced to keep terrorists from using coded e-mail.

# Who Are the Hackers?

Cyber criminals can cause a tremendous amount of damage. Why on earth would anyone want to become one?

There are several kinds of **hackers.** There are those who hack to steal money or goods. Some are employees who are angry at their bosses or their companies, and set out to cause damage or leak secrets. And there is another group of people who just like cracking computers to show off, or to deliver messages about things they believe in. Even those who simply want to show off can cause a lot of damage.

## The case of Raphael Gray

Nineteen-year-old Raphael Gray was a computer enthusiast from a small town in Great Britain. Gray read about a weakness in some computer **software** used by several **online** stores, which meant that it would be possible for him to obtain the **credit card** numbers that customers had used on the sites. He could then use the card details to go shopping.

Gray used the weakness to break into the online stores, and stole the details of 25,000 credit cards. Instead of keeping them all to himself, he posted the details of 6,000 cards on a website. Anyone who looked at that website could have used the information. Gray also used the card of a man named Bill Gates to send prescription drugs to the famous Bill Gates, chairman of Microsoft, as a joke.

The credit card companies found out about Gray's **scam,** however, and spent $3 million refunding customers whose cards were misused and issuing replacement cards.

Hacker Onel de Guzman was a suspect in the "ILOVEYOU" **virus** case. This virus stole computer users' passwords and e-mailed them to others, affecting thousands of people around the world.

16

The FBI was alerted to Gray's activities, and he was quickly caught. Despite his boasting on Internet **chat rooms** that he was a skilled hacker, the investigators had found it easy to trace his address. Early one morning the police raided his home, where he lived with his parents, and Gray was arrested. He pleaded guilty to breaking into computer systems in the United States, Britain, and Canada in order to "obtain services by deception." He was sentenced to three years of community service, with an order to seek psychiatric help.

Gray did not make any personal gain from his crimes, but the cost to others, such as credit card companies and online stores, was huge. The card users were also affected, with a great deal of worry and wasted time. A spokesman for one of the credit card firms affected by Gray's crimes summed it up: "This is not a victimless crime," he said.

A technical expert with the Philippines National Bureau of Investigation displays a computer disk seized from the apartment of Onel de Guzman.

# Friend or Foe?

Raphael Gray, like other cyber criminals, cost businesses millions of dollars, and caused problems for thousands of **credit card** users with his cyber attacks. Gray says he did not set out to do this. His plan, he claimed, was to draw attention to security problems in popular **software** in order to stop other cyber criminals from carrying out more serious crimes.

Many cyber criminals say this when they are caught, or when talking about their actions. They say that what they are doing is not for their own gain, but to improve security and embarrass software makers. There is fierce debate between people who believe that what these "friendly **hackers**" do can be justified, and those who say all such behavior is wrong.

For instance, one "friendly hacker" in the United States has discovered several major security flaws at big companies. The twenty-year-old will break into a computer system and then tell the company about what he has done, so they can fix the hole he discovered. He does not attempt to steal from the companies he breaks into, or encourage others to do so, but he is still breaking the law. The only time hacking can be legal is when companies hire skilled hackers to try and break into their systems to see if there are any weak spots. Some former hackers, such as John Draper, now turn their expertise to helping big companies keep the hackers out.

Others commit cyber crime not for the money, but simply for the recognition they gain. Movies, and the notoriety of big-name hackers, make cyber crime look glamorous to some. And many believe that it's not as serious as crime committed in the "real world." There is also a strong community of hackers who boast to each other about their exploits and swap tips. Some even create software to make hacking into other computers easy. All these things can make cyber crime seem less serious than it really is.

This teenage hacker, known as "Coolio," was just sentenced to nine months jail time in New Hampshire. He pleaded guilty to hacking into national computer sites belonging to the Army and the Air Force.

# Kevin Mitnick

The most notorious hacker in the world is Kevin Mitnick. He started his criminal career when he was only seventeen, and is seen as a hero by some would-be cyber criminals. In 1989 he was convicted of stealing software and codes for long-distance telephone lines, and was sent to prison for a year. Five years later, after using his skills to create several fake identities and staying on the run for two years, he was caught again. He was charged with several crimes, including stealing 20,000 **credit card** numbers and secret plans from several companies. This time his sentence included five years in prison, with eight months in solitary confinement, and a long ban on using computers.

**❝I am not innocent but I certainly didn't do most of what I was accused of. A hacker doesn't deliberately destroy data or profit from his activities. I never made any money directly from hacking. I wasn't malicious.❞**

(Kevin Mitnick, quoted in *Wired News*, October 2001)

Kevin Mitnick was released from jail in 2000.

# Creating Havoc: The Organized Groups

Not all organized groups of cyber criminals are breaking the law to make money. Like some **hackers** who work alone, some groups just want to see if they can cause chaos and get noticed.

One hackers' group has released computer programs that make it possible to control other people's **PCs** across the Internet, without the computers' owners being aware that their computers are being accessed. Despite the fact that the program allows hackers to break the law by using another person's computer without permission, it is a matter of pride for its makers that they have managed to exploit this security hole.

Other groups have created programs and websites that make it possible to create a working **credit card** number. This number might be one that belongs to someone already, or it might be one that has not yet been allocated. Programs and websites such as these encourage others to break the law by making cyber crime easier.

This website was hacked by "Analyzer," an Israeli hacker.

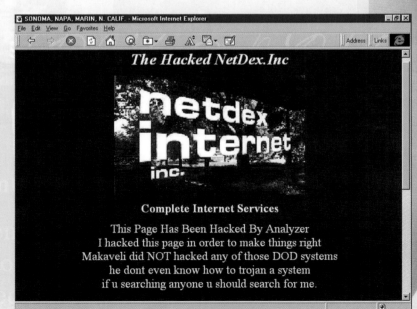

SONOMA, NAPA, MARIN, N. CALIF. - Microsoft Internet Explorer

File Edit View Go Favorites Help

Address | Links

*The Hacked NetDex.Inc*

**netdex internet inc.**

**Complete Internet Services**

This Page Has Been Hacked By Analyzer
I hacked this page in order to make things right
Makaveli did NOT hacked any of those DOD systems
he dont even know how to trojan a system
if u searching anyone u should search for me.

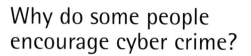

# Why do some people encourage cyber crime?

The creators of programs and websites such as this argue that, by doing so, they are exposing the poor security of popular **software** or credit cards. Like the "friendly hackers" discussed earlier, these groups say they are performing a service.

This may sometimes be true and, certainly, a number of security holes have been closed as software companies, such as Microsoft, and the credit card companies work to make their security better. However, it can also be argued that the hacker groups have other, less honorable motives. When they expose another "exploit" (a term hackers use for the security holes they find), they get the credit for the discovery. Gaining the admiration and praise of friends and colleagues is important. Especially for members of hacker groups where the only way most members know each other is through their "exploits."

Eighteen-year-old Ehud Tenebaum ("Analyzer"), from Israel, spent eleven hours being questioned by police over a cyber assault on the Pentagon's computer systems.

# The Superhighway Robbers

Imagine a cyber criminal and you might think of a nerdy young man or woman, sitting in a dark room, spending all of his or her time on the computer. It is certainly easier to imagine a few lone individuals wanting to create havoc on the Internet than entire groups.

Even so, just as with crime in the "real" world, some of the biggest cyber crimes have been pulled off by groups of people, working together and combining their abilities to reach their goal. That goal might be to encourage widespread hacking, steal a lot of money, or spread chaos through a **virus.**

# The Citibank robbery

For instance, in 1994 a Russian gang carried out the first known "**network robbery**" of a bank. Vladimir Levin, a young **hacker,** used his skills to access Citibank's computer network and steal a list of customer codes and passwords. He then logged into the network 18 times over several weeks, and moved $3.7 million from victims' bank accounts to other accounts around the world that were operated by the gang.

The crime was noticed when customers realized money was disappearing from their accounts, and complained to the bank. The international police force, Interpol, managed to trace Levin to London, and he was eventually jailed for three years. Four members of the gang admitted conspiracy to commit bank **fraud** and were also punished.

This crime proved a couple of things that hadn't been thought of before.

First, banks realized they were now targets for a new breed of criminal— the cyber criminal. They would have to tighten up their security in order to look after their customers.

Second, Levin was not working by himself. He was part of a gang that had carefully masterminded the crime. Had they succeeded, it would have been one of the biggest bank robberies in history, and it took place without a single shot being fired.

The nature of the Internet, and the number of people connected to it, means that crimes carried out by cyber criminals could claim more victims than ever before. For most people the chances of being robbed in the street are very low. If cyber crime were allowed to grow, the chances of being affected by crime could suddenly become much higher.

# Credit Card Crime Explained

When we hear about cyber criminals breaking into websites, we usually learn that they are doing it to steal **credit card** information. Why?

The first reason is that every **online** shop holds lots of credit card details in its computers. Nine out of ten purchases over the Internet are paid for with a credit card. Without credit cards, we would have to use other methods that would not be nearly as convenient—like writing a check, or transferring cash from one bank to another. Credit cards make online shopping very fast and easy, but because of this, the computers that hold all of a website's customer information are also the cyber criminals' first targets.

The second problem is the way credit cards work. Because credit cards were designed many years ago, long before the Internet, they are easy for cyber criminals to defraud. Once a cyber criminal has a stolen credit card number, it is possible for him or her to buy things online instantly.

# How do credit cards work?

Credit cards allow eligible people to pay for things without needing to carry lots of cash.

The customer is given a plastic credit card issued by a company such as MasterCard or Visa. These companies have agreements with stores around the world. Each store pays a small fee for every payment it takes with a card.

Each credit card carries a unique number and the customer's signature on the back. When the customer wants to buy something using a card, the store copies the card, including the unique number, and asks the customer to sign a slip of paper. The signature on the slip of paper is checked against the signature on the back of the card—if they match, the store knows the person making the purchase is also the card owner.

Credit cards were designed long before the **World Wide Web** existed and, over the Internet, signatures cannot be matched. This means that all a cyber criminal needs in order to buy something online is a stolen credit card with a name, number, and the expiration date.

This means credit card companies are now looking at other ways to make sure that the shopper is also the cardholder, which might help stop credit card cyber crime. These include individual pin numbers to be entered with other details, putting special microchips in the cards, and only sending goods to the billing address, instead of having them shipped to a separate delivery address.

# A Victimless Crime?

This book has already looked at some of the damage cyber crime does. But how does this affect ordinary people? After all, the banks are the ones losing all the money when cyber criminals attack. Big companies have to pick up the bill if **viruses** bring down the Internet. And **credit card** companies protect their customers, which means the cardholder does not have to pay if he or she is the victim of **fraud.**

All this is true, but it is still ordinary people (citizens, shoppers, and computer users) who eventually pay the price for cyber crime. The problem lies in the way victims of crime—computer users, shops, and other businesses—recover after criminals have struck.

# Spreading the cost

For example, many people buy insurance, meaning that they make a regular payment to an insurance company to protect their belongings. Then if they lose something through theft or accident, the insurance company pays for the stolen or damaged goods to be replaced. The insurance companies make money, because many more people buy insurance than are the victims of crime or accidents.

However, if more people become victims of cyber crime, the insurance companies will have to pay out more money. That means they will have to charge all their customers more in order to pay for the increased number of claims. Because insurance companies often insure a range of things—from bicycles to whole warehouses—the monthly amount for everything is likely to go up. If there was a wave of cyber crime, even someone who had never used the Internet could end up helping to pay for crimes committed on it.

The same problem exists in other areas, too. If a cyber criminal uses a credit card, the card company will make sure the card's real owner does not have to pay the bill. In the past the credit card company would meet the cost itself, paid for by the money it charges its customers to use the cards, or through fees charged to stores.

However, once the card companies realized the bill for cyber crime could be huge, they changed the rules. Today the same card companies do not pick up the bill for crime themselves. Instead, they pass it back to the online stores. In order to make sure they have some spare money on hand to pay the bill for credit card fraud, stores have to raise their prices. In this way we all end up paying for cyber crime.

Many **online** stores also exist in the real world. The biggest names in our shopping malls usually have big websites, and that creates another problem. What happens if one of these major chain stores is hit by cyber crime? Imagine if a major chain store's website was closed down by cyber criminals. It would mean the huge warehouses holding stock would be lying unused. Whole buildings full of customer service representatives would be silent, and delivery vans would be standing still.

The cost to the whole business—not just the Internet part—would be huge, because all these people and all these buildings would still have to be paid for, whether they were working or not. When businesses are faced with big losses, they often have to cut jobs. People become unemployed, shareholders in the company see their dividends (share of profits) fall, and the service to all of us gets poorer.

# The lasting effects

The side effects of cyber crime last long after the problems created by the criminals themselves have been fixed. Today, many people are still worried about buying things over the Internet, because they fear their **credit card** may be misused. When people read in newspapers or see on TV that a retail cyber crime has taken place, two things may happen. First, their confidence in online shopping is shaken, and they are less likely to use the Internet to shop. Second, if a particular online store has been the victim of cyber criminals, shoppers are likely to avoid buying from it. Because of these overall effects, online stores are less likely to make a profit, and customers might be denied many of the good things about online shopping, such as having a wide selection, being able to find discounts, and the convenience that shopping from home offers. It can also spell disaster for the online business— lost profits, more job cuts, even the closing down of services we all find useful. Even if cyber criminals do not directly touch us, they can still indirectly affect our lives.

# Virus victims

**Viruses** can wreak havoc on any computer. Many are designed only to copy themselves, but if they are not well written, they can cause computers to crash, frustrating users and erasing their work. More vicious viruses are designed to cause damage. The ILOVEYOU virus, which affected hundreds of thousands of computers from around the world in 2000, stole users' secret passwords and e-mailed them to an anonymous e-mail address. Others can wipe out **hard disks,** copy private files to strangers, or cause computers to behave strangely.

> **"**It's seemingly easier to commit fraud over the Net ... bigger stores are easiest to hit because some of the smaller stores are more scrutinizing and verify more detail.**"**
>
> (A cyber criminal quoted by *News.com*)

Employees of a Japanese provider of tools to detect and block viruses give advice to users in May 2000. Tens of thousands of Japanese returned to work after a public holiday to find the "ILOVEYOU" virus waiting in their e-mail.

# Credit Card Fraud Victims

There have been many victims of **credit card fraud,** but the most frequent victims are the **online** stores. Credit cards were designed to be used face to face. Online stores, though, operate in a "virtual" world, where they cannot see the person making the purchase. That means they are much easier targets for cyber criminals.

## Online companies

It is difficult to get exact details of how many online stores have been damaged by cyber crime, because some do not want to admit they have been hit for fear of driving away customers. But surveys show that only half of all businesses see the Internet as a safe place to buy and sell goods and services. There is certainly no doubt that many online businesses have been recent victims of cyber crime.

Some companies even make the claim cyber crime has forced them to go out of business. Flooz.com, a website endorsed by actress and comedian Whoopi Goldberg, went out of business in 2001. Flooz.com was an online gift certificate site where users could buy "Flooz points" to give as presents to friends and family. The points could be spent at various online stores.

Just months before Flooz went out of business, police were called in when it was alleged that a ring of cyber criminals from Eastern Europe had used stolen credit card details to buy Flooz points. Banks immediately stopped all payments on goods bought using Flooz points, and a million dollars of the company's money was held, just in case there were more bills for goods purchased with stolen points. In the end the company had to pay $300,000 (on top of the million that was being held) for goods bought using the stolen Flooz points.

Customers continued to spend their Flooz points. But with a big chunk of their money frozen, the company had to close its website in August 2001, saying credit card fraud had played a part in its problems. Many users were upset that they could no longer use the Flooz points they had received as gifts or even paid for themselves.

Cyber criminals have almost forced other **e-commerce** sites out of business in this way, and there is now great pressure on the credit card companies to think of ways to solve the problem.

# Individual victims

Credit card fraud is a real problem for ordinary
people, as well. Victims only find out about the
crime when their bill shows purchases they have
not made. They then have to call their credit card
company and try to prove they did not buy these
things. An investigation is launched, and a new
card must be issued. In the end a victim should
not have to pay directly for the fraud. However,
he or she will spend a good deal of time clearing
up the problem (and worrying about it). There are
fears that if this type of fraud is not stopped,
people will be reluctant to use their credit cards
on the Internet.

Attorney General Janet
Reno and Rubin Garcia,
assistant director of the
FBI, announced the
creation of the Internet
Fraud Complaint Center
in May 2000. It was set
up to tackle the growing
problem of Internet fraud.

# Software: Functions Versus Flaws

Some cyber criminals target the **software** used on computers. Modern programs often include lots of time-saving features designed to make users' lives easier. For example, functions called **macros** can carry out boring or repetitive tasks, while e-mail address books mean users don't have to memorize the addresses of every person they know.

## Worms

Cyber criminals have come up with a special kind of **virus,** called a worm, to attack these pieces of software. Like a real earthworm, this program can duplicate itself. It sends copies of itself over a network, and then the copies send copies of themselves, and so on.

This kind of virus creates a big problem for Internet users. A worm will often use the macro function built into popular software to copy itself to everyone in a user's address book. If they have stored a lot of addresses, it means a lot of e-mail is going to be sent out very quickly without their permission. If many computers do this all at the same time, it can over-burden the Internet, causing it to work more slowly or even shut down.

**❝In some ways, I'm surprised that they haven't brought down the Internet.❞**

(Robert Graham of the computer security company, Network ICE, talking to *News.com* about Internet worms)

# What can be done?

There is an ongoing debate in the computer industry about how to tackle this kind of cyber crime. Some say that big software companies like Microsoft have added new features to their software without thinking about security concerns. Critics say software writers should be forced to think about how to make their software safe for the Internet, instead of simply thinking of new things to sell to customers.

The software companies argue that they are trying to close security holes. Viruses that take advantage of their software are embarrassing for these companies. At the same time, they also want their software to be as easy to run as possible, because the average computer user is easily intimidated by complicated programs. The software companies also say that if they do not add new features to software, it becomes more difficult to sell new versions.

Virus creator Chen Ing-hau
provides an antivirus program
during a police interrogation
in Taiwan.

# Music On the Internet

One big area of discussion surrounds **online** music and video. For some time, it has been possible to get free copies of songs or films through online services that allow computer users to swap files.

The first of these services was called Napster. At its peak Napster allowed millions of people to swap **MP3** files for free. One person could buy a CD, use a computer to make an MP3 file of it, and swap this file for another he or she hadn't bought. This way the person got two CDs for the price of one. Napster users didn't have to spend much money to have all of the music they wanted.

What people were doing on Napster was actually illegal: by making MP3 files and sharing them with anyone, they were **pirating** music, which meant that the recording artists and their record companies were not being paid for their work. This version of Napster was eventually shut down after a series of court cases, although the Napster name lives on through a legal, paid membership-based music service.

However, there are still ways for Internet users to share their music collections, and record companies have experimented with ways to stop them. Not all of these experiments have been popular.

For instance, one of their first ideas was to make CDs that could only be played on normal CD players, and not on the CD players in computers, so computer users would no longer be able to make MP3 copies of their CDs. But this was unpopular with many people who were used to and enjoyed playing music through their computers. Others argued that copyright laws allowed them to make a single copy of a CD they had bought if it was only for their own use.

Another way that record companies have tried to cut down on pirating of music was by using special encoding on their CDs that made the music more difficult to copy. Users claimed that this made it harder for them to enjoy the music on different devices, such as portable MP3 players.

## Striking a balance

There is an ongoing debate between music companies and their customers. Record labels want to protect their businesses. If people expect music for nothing, the record companies will not have enough money to pay their musicians or find new ones. On the other hand, it might be harmful for record labels to upset their customers too much by clamping down on copying, and it might even encourage people to break the law. Furthermore, their are some supporters of music sharing who believe that by allowing people free access to music, they will be able to discover performers they had not been exposed to before. If they like what they hear, they will be inspired to purchase the recording.

The Napster website displays a news flash about its music-sharing services.

# The Law Versus Freedom

Cyber crime comes in many different forms, and all of them can cause damage to Internet users and businesses. Yet, officers of the law have a difficult time dealing effectively with cyber crimes.

Aren't the laws strong enough? Maybe not. There are several problems for the politicians who have to make decisions about rules and laws.

Sergeant Mark Lauer searches confiscated computers in Vermont. Police are now having to deal with computer crime including child pornography, business fraud, and e-mail harassment.

## Free speech and privacy

The main challenge is to balance public safety against the right to privacy and freedom of expression. For example, the public values the right to send and receive private messages without government interference. However, there is much controversy about the right to use secret computer coding, known as **encryption,** over the Internet. This is because the technology is so advanced that criminals can use it to hide their dangerous plans from the police.

In the case of free speech, any law that would restrict it has to be very carefully thought out, or the law itself could be illegal. For example, in the late 1990s there were plans in the United States to restrict the kind of material (especially **pornography**) that could be placed on the Internet.

Opponents managed to stop this because they argued that the laws would have restricted freedom of expression. They argued that if a law was introduced to restrict one kind of Internet material, it would be much easier from then on to introduce laws to shut down other kinds of websites. Websites, they argued, should not be closed or censored just because some people disagree with what they show.

# International boundaries

The second difficulty in creating new laws for the Internet is that the Internet travels freely across international borders, while most laws do not. In some countries, laws on Internet use are more relaxed. This might be because the Internet is not popular enough in a particular country for it to have created new laws. It could also be that such laws are not seen as a priority. This has a big effect on the Internet as a whole. Criminals can log on to the Internet from any country without solid cyber crime laws and attack computers many thousands of miles away without fear of punishment.

There are plans to create more international laws to fight cyber crime. However, such agreements (called **treaties**) take time to organize and discuss.

Detective Sergeant Tim Lee, of the CID Computer Crimes Unit in Michigan, investigates an alarming number of cyber crimes.

# The Rise of the Security Industry

What can be done to stop cyber criminals? Just like in the real world, where we use better locks and sturdier doors to keep out intruders, the virtual world of the Internet has tried to improve its security. In fact, a whole new industry has been created to help make the Internet a safer place.

First of all, individual users have been encouraged to take more responsibility for their **online** safety. Most of us would not leave our front doors unlocked, but until recently, many people had been putting their computers on the Internet without giving security a second thought.

Now that more computer users know about the dangers of **viruses,** more people are installing special virus protection **software** that filters everything the computer receives (including e-mail) and can remove any viruses it recognizes.

**"There are fourteen-year-old kids out there who can do things well beyond what someone with a computer science degree would dream of."**

(John Klein, from the company Rent-A-Hacker)

## Firewall protection

Computer users are also being encouraged to install special **firewall** software. A firewall is a computer program that works kind of like a bouncer at a nightclub. Every bit of information coming into the computer from the Internet is checked. If it does not seem suspicious, it is allowed through. Anything that looks dangerous is blocked, and the user is alerted.

A typed conversation between hackers is intercepted by the Honeynet Project.

Lance Spitzner founded the Honeynet Project. It has become one of the leading organizations that monitor the activities of computer hackers. A team of about 30 receives phone messages when computer networks under observation are being attacked.

## Changing sides

Surprisingly, many of the people joining this new industry are former **hackers** who have decided to use their computer skills to protect others. The help that these reformed cyber criminals provide is particularly valuable. Not only are they skilled computer users, but they also understand how hackers think. By asking themselves "What would I do in this situation?," they can often close a gap in security before it is found in public.

Even the most famous phone phreaker, John Draper, also known as "Captain Crunch," now runs his own business called Webcrunchers, a computer security company. Businesses are especially eager to get specialized help and advice on security. It often comes as a surprise to employers that one of the biggest risks they could face is having a disgruntled employee attempt to damage computer systems or destroy important files.

**❝Once a virus is out there it can't be reclaimed, so we wouldn't hire a former virus writer, because the damage from a virus is never-ending.❞**

(Jimmy Kuo, of anti-virus company McAfee)

# Selling Security

The biggest challenge for **online** stores, the most likely targets for cyber crime, is to make sure that information about customers is safe from the prying eyes of **hackers.** They must also reassure customers that they are truly safe.

As already discussed, many people have read about **credit card fraud** in newspapers, or seen stories about it on TV, so it has been difficult to persuade them that their information will be safe when shopping. Surveys prove that it takes a long time for Internet users to become confident in using their credit cards for purchases over the Internet.

## Staying safe

The best stores go to great lengths to prove they are safe to use. For example, Amazon.com, the biggest online store there is, points out that millions of customers have shopped with them without credit card fraud taking place.

In several places on their website, Amazon.com reminds customers that it uses Secure Sockets Layer (SSL) technology, an accepted way of **encrypting** (scrambling) messages between computers. Amazon goes on to explain that if fraud were ever to occur, the credit card companies would protect them for all but the first $50 lost. Amazon would even pay that for any **defrauded** customer who is not covered. And for those who are still too worried to give their credit card information online, Amazon offers a service that allows customers to complete purchases over the telephone.

Many other **e-commerce** sites have followed Amazon's lead, and some even use trusted consumer organizations to confirm independently that they have taken proper precautions.

All this activity ensures that security is tight between the shopper and the online store, and it allows customers to feel comfortable sharing their credit card information over the **World Wide Web.**

Online stores aren't the only ones that want customers to feel safe. The credit card companies themselves are exploring new ways to make their cards more secure. For example, some card companies are offering "one use" card numbers, which can only be used to buy things once. The challenge for everyone—stores, computer users, and credit card companies—is to stay one step ahead of the cyber criminals.

Takeshi Matsunobu, President of Sony Finance International, announces in Tokyo in 2001 that the Sony Corporation will offer a new credit card loaded with a computer chip to make Internet shopping easier and more secure.

# Fighting Cyber Crime

No matter how tight security is, there will always be cyber criminals trying to get through. Some of them, no doubt, will. This is why so much effort is spent finding new ways to catch cyber criminals.

One of the first lessons police forces learned is that, when it comes to cyber crime, national borders no longer exist. It is just as easy (or difficult) for a **hacker** based in Moscow to raid an American bank over the Internet as it is for a hacker in New York to do so.

## International cooperation

Because of the lack of international borders, police forces from different countries have to work closely together to fight cyber crime. This is not easy because, as was discussed before, each country has different laws, and what is illegal in one country might be allowed in another.

But on several important issues, including fraud, illegal content, and illegally copied **software,** most countries in the world agree. The case of Vladimir Levin and the Russian gang who robbed Citibank in 1994 was solved by police forces around the world working together. Interpol, an international police organization helped coordinate police action during this case. Now Interpol has parties working on cyber crime across the world. They bring together experts from around the world to offer advice and help each other out.

There have also been attempts to create an international **treaty** on cyber crime—a set of laws that would apply to most of the Internet-using countries in the world. International treaties, however, take time to discuss because of the large number of countries involved. There is also a great deal of opposition to the idea of such a treaty. Some people believe these new laws would harm civil rights and destroy some of the best things about the Internet.

One possible outcome of having such a treaty is that it could become much more difficult to do things on the Internet without revealing your full identity. This would help cut down on **fraud,** but it would also make it difficult for important services, like **online** support groups, to exist. These can carry out important services, such as giving teenagers an outlet to talk honestly about their problems at home or school, without fear of being identified by friends, teachers, or parents.

A hacker known as "Mudge" testifies before
a U.S. Senate Committee. He told the committee
that computer security is so poor, hackers could
disable the entire Internet in a half-hour.

# Media Focus

"Cyber zombies" sound more like something out of a bad horror film than something that could actually exist in the real world. Yet the *Sun Herald*, an Australian newspaper, warned of an attack of the "cyber zombies" in October 2000, telling readers that they are serious, and could potentially cause billions of dollars in damages. Cyber zombies are said to be **viruses** that, once inside a computer, wait for a certain date to trigger them. However, cyber zombies have yet to appear.

Meanwhile an alert issued by the FBI, about a new Internet worm called "Code Red," made headlines on television networks around the world, including CNN. It was feared that the virus would bring down the Internet in only a few hours but, in fact, it didn't have much effect at all.

These are just two examples of the huge amount of coverage given to cyber crime since the Internet became popular, and both show how newspapers and television can sometimes make potential problems seem far worse than they actually are.

Both of these stories caused a great deal of concern. With any virus scare, businesses spend time and money checking their systems. Scares, even if later proved to be exaggerated, can create fears that the Internet is not a safe place to spend time or do business.

## EXPERT WARNS OF ATTACK OF THE CYBER 'ZOMBIES'

**By John Hampshire, Technology Writer**

A global expert on cybercrime, Chris Rouland, warns that thousands of Australian computers have been infected with zombies ready to launch attacks that will cripple commercial sites such as Amazon.com, costing operators millions of dollars. His warning comes as new data shows fraud costs Australia more than $3 billion a year.

Beware, Australia, the zombies are out to get you. But don't laugh, because this is billion-dollar serious. Zombies are programs that lie dormant until they're told to cripple computers with huge amounts of bogus data.

The e-crime report released by the Australian Centre for Policing Research also says latest estimates are that $960 billion in illicit cash is laundered globally each year. Hacker and fraud attacks are swamping authorities.

An alarmist warning about a possible virus attack appeared in the *Sun Herald*, Australia, October 29, 2000.

# Putting things in perspective

Stories about cyber crime are, in many cases, exaggerated. Cyber crime is a very new area. Many people do not know a lot about computers, or how the Internet works, so they are more likely to worry about things that are not all that serious.

For example, there has been very little crime committed against people who are buying things using a secure **web server.** Most crimes happen when **credit cards,** or the numbers on them, are stolen from somewhere else.

And as with anything new, a great deal of hype (over-the-top publicity) surrounds Internet security. There is certainly no shortage of "experts" (many of whom are interested in selling their own Internet security products) willing to tell a reporter that there are frightening new viruses on the loose. In today's movies and TV shows, **hackers** are portrayed as powerful, clever criminals who can crack any system, when in reality this is unlikely.

Once more people get used to the Internet and realize what the real dangers are, media coverage will improve and reflect what is really happening in the **online** world. And that might have a very positive side effect— once the misplaced mystique and glamour are removed from cyber crime, there probably won't be as many people tempted to break the law.

This still is from *Wargames*, a movie about a hacker who saves the world.

# How Not to Be a Cyber Criminal

One of the problems with the Internet is that it makes breaking the law very easy. Even something as simple and seemingly harmless as downloading illegal **MP3** music files off of the Internet makes someone a cyber criminal.

There are many places **online** where people can pick up the latest chart hits for nothing, although record companies are always working to get laws passed that could close down these services.

It is in your best interest to avoid downloading any music from the Internet unless you download from a site that is endorsed by a record company. Some pirate sites could infect your computer with a **virus.** Also, your illegal download of music can lead to record companies raising prices of store-bought music as well as the music available on legitimate music sites.

# Illegal hacking

Another easy way to break the law is to try **hacking** into computer systems. Some people do not realize that just attempting to get into a computer or Internet account by guessing the password is a cyber crime, and in many countries it is just as illegal as the kind of hacking carried out by professional hackers like Kevin Mitnick. You are unlikely to go to jail for guessing a password, but breaking into an account could get you disconnected from the Internet, not to mention cause you embarrassment. Your school or your Internet provider will have rules on what users can (and cannot) do.

Finally, be careful about what you download and send to your friends on the Internet. Files you might think are funny or interesting may be seen by others as annoying or offensive, or they may be passing on viruses to your friends' computers. The safest thing to do is to check the rules and laws on what you can look at on the Internet, and what you can keep stored on your machine. If you are in any doubt about material, it is safer not to download it, and definitely avoid sending it to others.

# Internet Safety Checklist

## On your computer

- Make sure your computer is secure with up-to-date **virus** protection software. You can find a basic one for free **online** or buy more advanced protection at a computer store. Follow the maker's instructions for keeping the antivirus software up to date.

- If you use a shared computer at school or in an Internet cafe, do not use the "remember password" option that is available on some websites. Other people will be able to get in and pretend they are you!

- When using shared computers, always close any open **browser** windows and log off after you have finished.

- Make it hard for the **hacker.** If you have a cable modem or other "always on" Internet connection (one where you don't dial up) it is a very good idea to install a **firewall** program. This is like a locked front door for your computer. Again, you can get these free online or buy one at your local computer store.

- Do not use someone else's login, even if you are sure they won't mind.

## On the Internet

- Be careful in **chat rooms:** people may not be who they say they are.

- Never arrange to meet someone you have met over the Internet.

- Never give out personal information like your address or phone number.

- Think twice about sharing **MP3** music collections with other people, or downloading music from unofficial Internet services. If you share or download copyrighted music, you could be breaking the law.

- Remember, it is your responsibility to know what you are allowed to do on the Internet. Never be tempted to break the rules, because it keeps getting easier to get caught.

## Online shopping

- Make sure you know how long it will take for delivery, and exactly what everything is going to cost before buying. Is there a postal address and a phone number for the company you are buying from? This means you can contact them if you have a complaint.

- Make sure the online store you want to use has secure ordering. Most browser programs will indicate that you are using an **encrypted** connection with a symbol, such as a key or padlock, in one of the status bars.

- Always print out the confirmation screen after you have ordered. It is proof of your order.

- Be cautious of online auctions, because items might not be as good as they seem. Only buy from people who have been recommended by other users.

## E-mail

- Do not open e-mail attachments unless you are sure what is in them, even if they come from someone you know.

- Only send attachments when it is really necessary. If an attachment is small enough, try to move its text into a message instead.

- Be suspicious of e-mail warning you of virus threats, especially those that urge you to send the warning to your friends. These warnings are almost always hoaxes. If you are worried, check out the database of hoaxes and real threats at your antivirus software maker's website.

- Never send abusive e-mail messages. To avoid doing this, you should never send e-mail when you are angry.

# Facts and Figures

## The threat within

In June 2001, 57 percent of all companies surveyed told Digital Research that their worst security breaches happened when their own employees accessed information they were not supposed to see.

According to Information Security magazine, **viruses** hit 88 percent of U.S. companies in 2001—despite 90 percent of these companies having virus protection software.

## The fear factor

In a poll for The Information Technology Association of America and Tumbleweed Communications Corp. (December 2001):

- 71 percent of respondents said they were "very" or "somewhat" concerned about Internet and computer security.

- 78 percent of respondents said they were either "very" or "somewhat" concerned that personal information held by the government could be misused.

- 74 percent expressed worries about terrorists using the Internet to launch cyber attacks against critical infrastructure. (37 percent said they were "very" concerned, while another 37 percent said they were "somewhat" concerned.)

# The growth of Internet crime

**CERT** defines an incident as an attempt (successful or not) to gain unauthorized access to a system or its data; and also a disruption or **denial of service (DOS).** One incident might involve a single computer, or thousands of computers. Here are the number of worldwide Internet security "incidents" reported each year:

| 1991 | 1992 | 1993 | 1994 | 1995 | 1996 | 1997 | 1998 | 1999 | 2000 | 2001 |
|------|------|------|------|------|------|------|------|------|------|------|
| 406 | 773 | 1,334 | 2,340 | 2,412 | 2,573 | 2,134 | 3,734 | 9,859 | 21,756 | 52,658 |

Source: CERT

Computer security costs the Australian department of defense $8 million ($4.5 million U.S.) a year. $1 million ($550,000 U.S.) of that was for a special team of "**hacker busters**" to prevent cyber attacks.

# Further Information

## Contacts

**CERT**
e-mail: cert@cert.org
**www.cert.org**
U.S. government organization that tracks
Internet security incidents.

**Consumer Federation of America**
1424 16th St NW
Suite 604
Washington, D.C. 20036
(202) 387-6121
**www.consumerfed.org**
The Consumer Federation of America takes
interest in the safety of children on the
Internet, as well as users' privacy as they
use Internet services.

**Department of Justice**
10th & Constitution Avenue NW
Criminal Division, (Computer Crime &
Intellectual Property Section)
John C. Keeney Building, Suite 600
Washington, D.C. 20530
**www.cybercrime.gov**
The Department of Justice's cyber crime
pages have a wealth of information on the
issue, and what is being done to fight it.

**Internet Fraud Complaint Center**
**www1.ifccfbi.gov**
A website run by the FBI and the National
White Collar Crime Center. It offers advice on
how to avoid Internet **frauds** and allows
**defrauded** computer users to file complaints.

**National Consumer League**
1701 K Street NW
Suite 1200
Washington, D.C. 20006
(202) 835 3323
e-mail: info@nclnet.org
**www.nclnet.org/shoppingonline/**

The National Consumer League's advice on
safe shopping **online** will be of use to
Internet users around the world.

The National Consumer League also runs a
good website on how to protect yourself
against Internet fraud.
**www.fraud.org/Internet/intset.htm**

**The National Infrastructure Protection Center**
J. Edgar Hoover Building
935 Pennsylvania Avenue NW
Washington, D.C. 20535-0001
**www.nipc.gov**

The National Infrastructure Protection Center
investigates cyber crime carried out abroad.
Its web pages are a useful source of further
information on cyber crime.

**Project Honeynet**
Non-profit research group of security
professionals that studies and shares
information on the activities of hackers.
**http://project.honeynet.org**

**Symantec**
A security firm that offers a useful virus
encyclopedia.
**http://securityresponse.symantec.com/**
**avcenter/vinfodb.html**

# Further reading

Graham, Ian. 2002. *The Internet Revolution.* Chicago: Heinemann Library.

Morgan, Sally. 2001. *Internet.* Chicago: Heinemann Library.

Thomas, Douglas and Brian D. Loader. 2000. *Cybercrime: Law Enforcement, Security and Surveillance in the Information Age.* New York: Routledge.

Verton. 2002. *Hacker Diaries: Confessions of Teenage Hackers.* Berkeley, CA: McGraw-Hill Osborne.

Winder, Davey. 2001. *The Internet Guide for Kids 1.0.* Guilford, CT: The Globe Pequot Press.

# Glossary

**browser**   software for accessing websites and displaying web pages, such as MS Internet Explorer and Netscape

**CERT**   Computer Emergency Response Team. U.S. government organization that tracks security incidents.

**chat room**   place on the Internet where you can "chat" with other people through your computer

**constitution**   set of important rules that say how a country should be run, and what rights should be protected

**credit card**   card from a credit card company authorizing the holder to buy goods on credit and pay for them later

**defraud**   to steal by deceiving the victim or pretending to be someone else

**denial of service (DOS)**   kind of cyber crime where many computers (sometimes because they are infected with a virus) send messages to a single computer on the Internet. Because the target receives so many messages, it can stop working.

**e-commerce**   buying and selling of goods over the Internet

**encryption**   method of scrambling the messages between computers so that they appear meaningless to anyone trying to intercept them

**firewall**   machine and/or a piece of software that protects a computer by keeping out certain types of messages sent over the Internet

**fraud**   act of deception or misrepresentation

**hacker**   someone who tries to gain unauthorized access to other people's computers

**hard disk/hard drive**   space (or memory) on a computer that stores all of its software and files

**macro**   small, easily-created computer program that carries out boring or repetitive tasks. Macros are built into most popular software.

**MP3**   type of music file that has been compressed (squashed) to make it easier to send over the Internet

**network**   collection of computers joined together so they can communicate with each other

**online**   when a computer is connected to the Internet

**personal computer (PC)**   computer small enough to fit on your desk

**pirating**   copying a piece of music, video, or software without the copyright owner's permission

**pornography**   graphic depiction of sexual activity

**scam**   scheme to defraud people

**software**   instructions (or programs) that run your computer, often stored in your hard disk

**treaty**   agreement between countries to follow the same law

**virus** software program that spreads from machine to machine without the computer user's permission

**web server** software that runs a website. It manages all the web pages and handles requests from browsers to read pages.

**World Wide Web** part of the Internet that is easy to navigate with the use of "web browsing" software

# Index